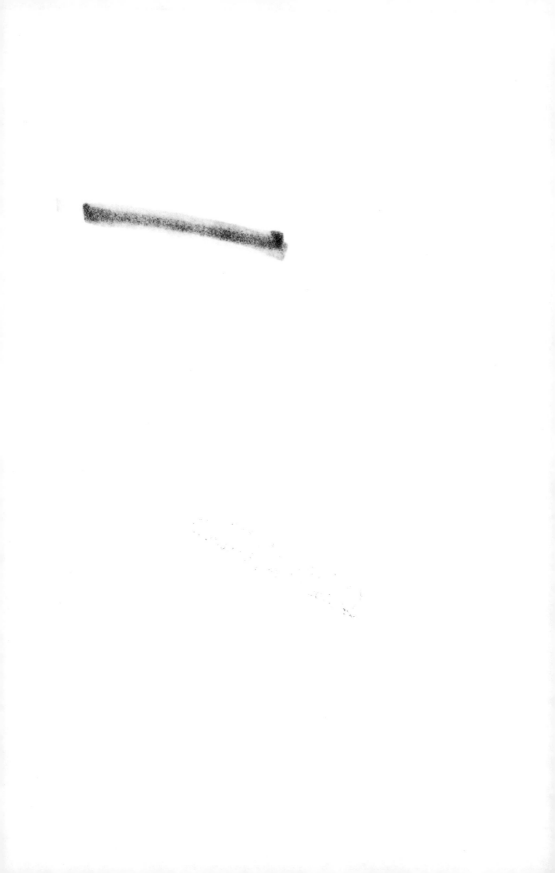

Everything
You Need to
Know About

The Riot Grrrl Movement: The Feminism of a New Generation

Riot Grrrls helped changed the face of popular feminism.

Everything
You Need to
Know About

The Riot Grrrl Movement: The Feminism of a New Generation

Chérie Turner

The Rosen Publishing Group, Inc.
New York

Published in 2001 by The Rosen Publishing Group, Inc.
29 East 21st Street, New York, NY 10010

First Edition

Library of Congress Cataloging-in-Publication Data

Turner, Chérie.
The riot grrrl movement: the feminism of a new generation / Chérie Turner.—1st ed.
p. cm. — (Need to know library)
Includes bibliographical references and index.
ISBN 0-8239-3400-4 (alk. paper)
I. Title. II. Series.
RC125 .P58 2000
616.9'14—dc21

00-010631

Manufactured in the United States of America

Contents

Punk rock was a natural environment for the start of the Riot Grrrl movement.

Introduction

Punk rock: loud, aggressive, rebellious, angry. The first image that comes to mind when you read those words is probably not of a teenage girl. Despite changing attitudes about women's roles in society, many people still believe that girls should be only pretty, polite, and not troublesome. But out of punk rock subculture sprang a group of teen girls and young women who embraced these punk sensibilities and changed the face of popular feminism. They called themselves riot grrrls.

Punk rock was born in the mid-seventies in New York City. It sparked the minds of youth the world over, but became especially popular in the bigger cities of the United States and England. It was music. It was fashion. It was politics. It became a lifestyle. One of the more lasting and inspiring elements of punk rock—especially among bored, working-class teens—was a "do it yourself" (DIY) philosophy, particularly in terms of music and fashion. Instead of listening to well-polished music, the idea was to get up on stage, bang out a few basic chords or drum beats, and shout confrontational lyrics. Be loud. Be angry. Have fun. Say something! Do something yourself.

In the early days of punk, men and women alike wrote, played, and performed. For the first time in the history of rock 'n' roll, women were almost as welcome to enter the arena as men. As noted in *Trouble Girls: The Rolling Stone Book of Women in Rock*, "Punk . . . allowed women to be nasty, aggressive, vitriolic [hostile], and outraged, to howl and roar and raise a ruckus." Chrissie Hynde, lead singer of the Pretenders and a part of the early London punk scene, states in Lauraine Leblanc's book *Pretty in Punk*, "The best things about [punk] for me was that I didn't have to rely on being a female guitarist as a gimmick . . . Punk allowed anyone in."

But as with most idealistic and liberating subcultures (groups that identify themselves as being outside the norm and thereby threaten established ways of society), it was not long before the influences of mainstream culture started to make their mark on the new movement. By the mid-1980s, men once again took over the punk music scene. The music had become "hardcore." To quote *Pretty in Punk*: "Once again, girls were

edged out of the bur- g e o n i n g [g r o w i n g] new hardcore punk scene. Never again would they occupy a central role in the punk subculture." The hardcore scene became violent and testosterone-fueled, and women were excluded. The dance floor, once a place where men and women alike jumped around, became a "mosh pit." In the pit, men violently collided into each other and women were groped, injured, or simply shoved to the side.

Then, states *Pretty in Punk* author Leblanc, "in the early 1990s, punk underwent yet another 'revival,' largely due to the popularity of 'grunge' . . . Punk had survived the conservative '80s, and in the late '80s and early '90s renewed itself in a variety of offshoots such as . . . Riot Grrrl." If women were no longer accepted as part of the group as they had been back in the late 1970s, they would now just create their own scene. The time had come for "Revolution, Grrrl-Style."

Chapter One

The Revolution

That second coming of punk, or grunge, in the late 1980s and early '90s, began in Olympia, Washington—home to the now infamous group that headlined the movement, Nirvana. Mixed in among that scene were a growing number of women. They were in bands—shouting powerful lyrics—and authoring fanzines, or 'zines (handmade magazines), which expressed their frustrations, creativity, emotions, and desires. But unlike their female punk rock predecessors who were embraced by the power structure of the subculture, these women were kept out of the limelight. And probably for this reason, these women differed from their predecessors in another important way: They were self-identified feminists.

The marginalization that these feminists faced only served to make them stronger, louder, more confrontational, and purposefully united. Slowly, they created a network of like-minded angry and outspoken women. Empowered by punk's DIY philosophy, they created a

Public protest was an integral part of the women's movement during the 1970s.

place for themselves by themselves. In a 1992 article for the *Chicago Reader*, Emily White observes: "Riot Girl [which these women would eventually call themselves] was started by a group of musicians and writers and friends who decided to aggressively co-opt the values and rhetoric of punk, fifteen years later, in the name of feminism."

These women were feminists, but not like those of their mothers' time. The once dynamic women's movement that had blossomed in the 1960s and 1970s seemed stale by the 1980s. For many, it was academic and usually identified with white, middle-aged women's groups. For these reasons, feminism was not a movement in which many younger women actively participated. This is echoed in one riot grrrl's July 2000 e-mail. She talks about her first encounter with Riot Grrrl: "Feminism before that point always felt like someone else's revolution. Something that happened in the '70s which was cool but it didn't have anything to do with me now in the '90s." The women in Olympia were breaking new feminist ground.

Combining the philosophies of feminism and punk proved to be powerfully effective. Women (and girls) dissatisfied with the status quo were empowered by the DIY, rebellious philosophy of punk. *Pretty in Punk* author Lauraine Leblanc recalls her own experiences in the early years of the scene. "Punk was, for me, the ultimate in self-empowerment in that I had moved from a position of victimization, as the smartest, dorkiest, most persecuted girl in school, to one of agency, as a person in control of my self-presentation."

Kathleen Hanna, lead singer of the hallmark (and now defunct) Riot Grrrl band, Bikini Kill, also points out the power of melding the punk ethic and feminism. In White's *Chicago Reader* article, Hanna "tells how the punk ethic helped make their kind of feminism possible. 'Something was happening in our community,' [Hanna] says. '[We realized] how important the whole punk you-can-do-anything idea was for women. It didn't matter if what the girls said was politically correct, or if they were good at their instruments; the point was simply to make some noise.' "

One of the founders of the Riot Grrrl movement was Kathleen Hanna, lead singer for Bikini Kill.

While mainstream feminists aimed to make women more powerful within the existing social structure, these punk feminists strove to create an entirely new structure. They sought to create power on women's terms by taking action, making things happen for themselves and each other. "I have met feminists where their whole thing is about getting ahead within the system the way it is," says Hanna in a 1998 interview for *Punk Planet* magazine. "They're still defining success in the same way it's always been defined—by money and how much control they can have over their environment . . . If we don't challenge the unhealthy forms of competitiveness that capitalism breeds, or the way it teaches us to objectify ourselves to each other, then we're just selling ourselves out . . . We need to at least create new structures and new ways of dealing with things." In the minds of punk feminists, women needed to launch a revolution.

Girl Day

This female faction of the grunge/punk scene grew rapidly. In 1991, recognizing the popularity of this movement, the organizers of the International Pop Underground (IPU) Convention in Olympia created Girl Day. This event was just the inspiration the women in this community needed to take hold of the powerful swell of new feminism they were generating with their aggressive music and 'zines. As noted in *Trouble Girls*: "After Girl Day . . . a revolutionary fervor took over Olympia, as a new breed of bands and activists became more confrontational and less cutesy about their gender politics . . . They called themselves 'grrrls,' with added defiance." Punk rock and feminism had officially joined forces. This volatile union proved powerful and unforgettable.

Starting the Riot

The woman credited with starting the Riot Grrrl movement is Kathleen Hanna. She led the revolution from the front of the stage, screaming, writing, and demanding that women be heard and that they share their experiences. And she was an unabashed feminist. "I wanted to make it really cool to be a feminist," Hanna says in Andrea Juno's *Angry Women in Rock.* "Because this was right when *Time* or *Newsweek* said that feminism was dead, around '89. Now everything is supposed to be 'post-feminist.' "

But Hanna was far from a one-woman crusade. Numerous women talked about feminist ideas and how they related to the punk scene, to pop culture, and to women in their teens and twenties. Tobi Vail, Bikini Kill's drummer, put out the 'zine *Jigsaw*, and Donna Dresch of the band Team Dresch created *Homocore*. Molly Neuman, the drummer of Bratmobile—another original Riot Grrrl band—summed up the feelings of solidarity that the Riot Grrrl movement generated in a November 15, 1992, *New York Times* article. "We were all talking about similar things . . . We were frustrated with the world and with sexism, and even with the sexism we saw in alternative culture. It was an exciting time for me, feeling like I wasn't crazy and there were people who felt the same things I did." These women undoubtedly realized something very profound was happening. And as they talked to each other more and more, these feelings of unity and shared purpose grew stronger.

The Meetings Begin

The revolution started to take shape after Bikini Kill and Bratmobile moved from Olympia to Washington, DC, home to many other feminist-minded bands and a large punk rock scene. Plans were put into action to create a fanzine in which these punk feminist thoughts could be discussed. "We were talking about starting a widely distributed fanzine," recalls Hanna in *Angry Women in Rock*. "So I said, 'Let's have a meeting about skill sharing.' We had the first meeting and about twenty women showed up. A lot of them had never been in a room with only women before and were blown away by what it felt like: Everybody had so much to say. That felt like an overwhelming response, so we continued our weekly meetings. And out of this, bands started, and fanzines ['zines] began . . . " At those meetings, they discussed various issues such as vegetarianism and sexism, released frustrations and anger, and shared experiences—especially experiences of sexual abuse. Their exchanges gave shape to a very strong feeling. And now it had a name that was often coupled with the slogan "Revolution, Grrrl-Style, Now!"

Action and Reaction

Riot grrrls began to hold meetings and conventions and create fanzines and bands. When these bands performed, the punk public got a real taste of what these women were putting together. One of the first public stances riot grrrls took was to reclaim their shows. In her 1992 *Chicago Reader* article, Emily White notes that "one of the most telling metaphors of the Riot

Bands like Bratmobile encouraged girls to confront sexism.

Grrrls is their dramatic invasion of the mosh pit . . . girls wanted a space to dance, so they formed tight groups and made their way to the front, protecting each other the whole way." Of this strong stance, Bikini Kill drummer Tobi Vail says, "Everything changed. Like at first when our band started, men could hardly deal with it. A really short time later, they came around and realized what we were doing was totally valid. In a really short time all these girls were being inspired by each other."

But not everyone embraced Riot Grrrl. There were plenty of negative reactions against this growing network of women. They were harassed and dubbed "man-haters," despite their motto "No we are not paranoid. No we are not man-haters." They were even threatened. As noted in *Trouble Girls*: "In the underground press, grrrls were getting bashed for being separatists, or just for being political at all." In *Angry Women in Rock*, Hanna adds, "I can't tell you how much opposition we experienced, and how much tension was out there . . . and sometimes even women didn't understand: 'Why do you have to have women-only meetings?' We said, 'Look it's only one hour a week. Every space is a male space—what's the problem?' "

Encouraged or not, Riot Grrrl moved forward and gained momentum. In fact, the resistance served only to make women like Hanna more determined. "It just showed how important what we were doing was, because people really hated it," Hanna claims in her *Angry Women in Rock* interview. Riot grrrls knew they were on to something important. But it was also clear that change would not happen overnight. Certainly, mainstream media and culture were not ready for this type of challenge to the status quo.

The Media Take Notice

The mainstream media, always hungry for controversial news and new trends, were quick to discover Riot Grrrl. Unfortunately, it soon became clear that the media could not understand or embrace such a radical and angry group of young women. The reaction was primarily negative, fear-based, and full of misinterpretations. As editor Barbara O'Dair explains in *Trouble Girls*: "Not surprisingly, *USA Today* and *Newsweek* didn't 'get it,' reducing revolution girl-style to a cute trend."

Some journalists did manage to cover the movement in a more accurate way. For example, *Seventeen* magazine reported that Riot Grrrl was "stomping out the sexist stereotypes of what girls are 'supposed' to be (quiet, sweet, quiet, soft, quiet—you get the picture)." But by and large, the mainstream media misrepresented the movement.

In the early days of Riot Grrrl, women were often misquoted and disrespected. Every opportunity was made to either destroy the movement or turn it into a manageable, teenybopper trend. Hanna recounts in *Punk Planet*: "The things I was saying . . . were very easily co-optible by capitalism and the mainstream media. They're very easily interpreted to mean, 'it's feminist to be really sexy for men.' That's not what I meant at all!" There was clearly little attempt to understand or take the movement seriously. The raw, angry attitude of Riot Grrrl was just too unladylike.

Riot grrrls were portrayed either as cutesy girls or as predators, a threat to "good girls." An article published by *Rolling Stone* in 1993 warned, "Like she-devils out of Rush Limbaugh's worst nightmare. They're called Riot Grrrls and they're coming for your daughters." *Punk Planet* noted that "even *Scholastic Update*, a trade magazine for teachers, included an article [about the movement] the main focus of which seemed to be how Riot Grrrl poses a threat to more 'traditional' girls organizations like Girl Scouts and the Future Homemakers of America."

These reactions were reminiscent of the way that punk rock was received in the early 1980s, when parents and law officials saw those involved in the scene as "degenerates." In response, organizations like Parents of Punkers and the Back in Control Training Center created programs that attempted to "depunk" teens. *Pretty in Punk* author Leblanc writes, "Most media coverage served only to reinforce the notion that punks are offensively, and even dangerously deviant . . . punks were demonized."

Some people challenged the sincerity of Riot Grrrl. In fact, publications like *Newsweek* simply questioned the seriousness of the girls' convictions in a 1992 article: "There's no telling whether this enthusiasm of the Riot Grrrls, their catchy passion for 'revolution, girl style,' will evaporate when it hits the adult real world."

Grrrls saw the media alter and repackage their powerful vision and they stepped up to protect it. White noted at the time: "After calls from *USA Today*, ABC News, Maria Shriver, and Maury Povich, they've instituted a press block . . . they've steadfastly refused to become fodder for the mainstream press." In a November 15, 1992, *New York Times* article, one young woman expressed her concern about media coverage: "Riot Grrrl is just something that's really important to me and I'm afraid of it being exploited."

Pop group the Spice Girls co-opted and commercialized some aspects of Riot Grrrl.

The Aftermath

In the end, media and marketing executives did manage to exploit aspects of the Riot Grrrl scene. They co-opted the style and language of Riot Grrrl, transforming politically and socially charged elements of the movement into marketable catch phrases. For instance, the term "girl power"—initially the title of an issue of Riot Grrrl fanzine *Bikini Kill*—became the slogan for the pop group the Spice Girls, a group that hardly embodied the type of independence and power Riot Grrrl promoted. As Carrie Brownstein, member of the band Sleater-Kinney, states in a June 18, 2000, *New York Times* article, Riot

21

Athlete Picabo Street was used to market "girl power."

Grrrl was "completely collapsed into the Spice Girls: T-shirts with 'Girls Rule' or 'Girl Power'—even if the Spice Girls would never know where it came from."

A 1997 *Village Voice* article notes how successfully the Spice Girls turned a serious movement into a capitalist's dream: "The Spice Girls have done the seemingly impossible: they have made feminism, with all its implied threats, cuddly, sexy, safe, and most important, sellable." In that same article, the *Voice* further notes the connection between Riot Grrrl and mainstream advertising: "Marketers seem to be betting their money on the rad femme (read: Riot Grrrl): Both Lady Footlocker and Mountain Dew have recently run commercials that showcase feisty but feminine girls." In describing the Mountain Dew commercial, they note that it is filled with "shots of lanky, raucous girls, and footage of wild women—young ski champion Picabo Street, a skydiver, a roller-blader attached to a helicopter—careening off dangerous precipices. As they take the plunge, they each let loose a savage girl-holler—the kind of roar you might hear in a Bikini Kill song, but stripped of anger and transformed into purely joyous exuberance." The media, it seemed, had just been handed the key to selling products to a young female audience. They took powerful Riot Grrrl concepts and reduced them to non-threatening, cute slogans.

Media attention also took its toll on the solidarity of the movement. In her 1997 essay "Media-Grrrl vs. Riot Grrrl," Lea Thomson contends, "I think the harm the media did was indismissable and pushed many away from the movement." She goes on to say that the women originally involved in the movement "were very disgusted with the media and became clique-ish. They assumed the newcomers only had ideas about Riot Grrrls from the media and wanted to take part because it was cool. They were harsh to outsiders and it stunted them badly." *Seventeen* echoes this observation. "Riot Grrrls are at odds on a number of issues. Like the punk superiority trip. 'I've gotten letters from girls saying they'd gone to meetings and people were hostile to them because they weren't really punk or militant,' Jessica (a former riot grrrl) says."

Despite these growing pains, the heart of Riot Grrrl had not been sold. It simply returned underground, out of the media spotlight. It would become recognized as an important step in empowering women of all ages. In fact, mainstream media would not take Riot Grrrl seriously until years later. It is now recognized by many as playing a very important role in empowering women. It has even been called the "third wave of feminism"—the first being the suffragist movement of the late nineteenth and early twentieth centuries, and the second being the women's liberation movement of the 1960s and 1970s. In her essay, "What Is Riot Grrrl Anyway?" riot grrrl "Spirit" insists, "Riot grrrls—the strongest, truest of us will outlast the trendiness."

Chapter Two

Grrrl Power

Riot grrrls called for united action, a revolution of girl power. But hadn't women in the United States gotten everything they'd been asking for? Did women still need to be fighting? Wasn't this a time of glorious opportunity for women?

That is how many people felt. But what price were women paying for their opportunity? Kathleen Hanna was keenly aware of the discrimination women continued to face, especially those working in the music industry. She comments in *Angry Women in Rock*, "I kept meeting women musicians and asking them questions like ... 'How does being female impact your work?' And everybody was going, 'Oh, it doesn't matter that I'm a woman; I'm a musician first.' And I was asking, 'Okay ... but isn't it weird that the guys in your band insist that you wear a tight dress and lipstick while they dress totally yucky on stage?' I was meeting women who were telling me stories like this, but in the next breath they'd say ... they transcended gender." The price of opportunity: a double standard. You can play, but you are allowed to do so only within the confines of the patriarchal social system.

Herein lies the central issue of Riot Grrrl: They called for opportunity, self-image, society, and life on female terms. And given the toll the current system of social constraints seemed to be taking on the self-esteem of many young women, it is not surprising that this idea was received so passionately.

Social Constraints and Girl Confidence

During adolescence, people begin to experience and experiment for the first time with adult roles. More than ever, gender begins to define identity. Teens often experience social constraints—the guidelines that dictate how to properly act, dress, speak, and identify oneself. Unfortunately, as Leblanc explains in *Pretty in Punk*, it has been shown that "as girls enter adolescence, they lose self-esteem in their attempt to conform to the constraints and demands of the female gender role." Leblanc continues: "In the attempt to model themselves to the impossible ideal of femininity, girls are asked to suppress positively valued attributes such as assertiveness, spontaneity, and self-possession in favor of attractiveness, docility, and passivity." Given that girls feel disempowered as they enter adulthood and mature into women, the idea of defining and

Riot grrrls, such as Team Dresch, celebrated individuality.

embracing female power seems critical for girls and women alike.

Riot grrrls sought to create a system in which girls dictate the social constraints. They wanted a system in which girls could just be themselves. In fact, a unique feature of Riot Grrrl was the age of the girls it attracted. As opposed to earlier forms of feminism, which often appealed to women college-age and older, Riot Grrrl attracted young women. "Sometimes girls as young as eleven come to our shows," Hanna states in *Angry Women in Rock*. "I think it's really cool that they feel included. It's like I achieved my goal; for some of those girls feminism really is cool now!" No doubt, Riot Grrrl gave frustrated young women something powerful with which to identify. As pointed out by Emily White, "After a while, this anger didn't feel like a fad, it felt like hope—compelling girls to organize weekly meetings, start calling themselves soldiers, messengers."

Spreading the Word

The message spread quickly. The troops of the revolution rallied enthusiastically. Grrrls were encouraged to talk to each other and share ideas, skills, and enthusiasm, and to find a unified voice. Fliers were passed out at shows that encouraged girls to talk to each other and unite. Hanna says, "I wrote, 'Go to shows! Write stuff on your hands and arms so that other women will know that you're into feminist stuff too, and they'll come talk to you and then maybe you can hang out.' " Soon enough, Riot Grrrl chapters popped up all over the United States.

What Were They Saying?

The central goal of Riot Grrrl was to create a new social structure that empowered women: a society in which women were truly free to be themselves and be strong. In issue #2 of *Bikini Kill*, riot grrrls outline some of the reasons for their revolt: "Because we must take over the means of production in order to create our own moanings. Because we are interested in creating non-hierarchical ways of being and making music, friends, and scenes based on communication + understanding, instead of competition + good/bad categorizations. Because we are angry at a society that tells us Girl = Dumb, Girl = Bad, Girl = Weak. Because we hate capitalism in all its forms and see our main goal as sharing information and staying alive, instead of making profits off being cool according to traditional standards."

Indeed, Riot Grrrl strongly rejected the destructive dictates of capitalism. Riot grrrls recognized the way in which capitalism creates unhealthy competitive

Girl Love Is . . .

* treating all girls with respect
* hugging your girlfriends and being there for them
* protecting each other and providing a feeling of
    safety when we walk down the street or go out
* making space where women/girls feel
    unthreatened and unintimidated
* talking about abuse and rape when
    no one else will listen
* making other girls feel unafraid to eat
    in public or around others
* making other girls feel comfortable with their bodies

* being kind to your mom and not expecting
    her to wait on you
* not judging women/girls on their looks
    and/or hating them for being pretty
* not competing for boys' attention
* not looking/acting dumb on purpose so
    boys will like you
* not picking your new boyfriend over your
    old girlfriends
* calling people on their opinions
* not feeling homophobic around your
    girlfriends and refusing to touch them
* learning and teaching each other how to do
    stuff and be active

* screaming in public
* knowing that girls can do anything
    boys can do
* stopping jealousy
* respecting the choice of girls to be sexually
    active or to abstain from sex

* knowing that you are connected to all girls
    and the way you view yourself is related
    to their self-image as well
* sharing resources with other girls
* helping each other see our beauty and
    build our own culture around
    what we see
* wearing makeup and tight clothes
    because we want to

* being powerful
* being honest and straightforward
    because mind games stink
* talking about our feelings
* holding hands
* feeling okay about being naked around each other
* understanding that girls that we may not like
    are people, too
* not letting certain words such as "feminist" be
    used as insults against people

relationships, in which people are interested in money more than other people's well-being. It objectifies people (especially women), defining them as items to be bought and sold rather than seeing them as people. And they were sadly aware of how corporate actions frequently destroy the environment. They also saw how capitalism allowed only for a narrow view of success, one based on acquiring and accumulating money.

And what would replace the current structure? That was for all the girls who joined the riot to decide. Riot grrrls understood social change as a long-term, ongoing process. "Part of the whole idea of Riot Grrrl was that you couldn't define it: each person defined it as it happened," states Hanna. "So when people would ask what it was, we couldn't say because we didn't know, because it was constantly changing. One week we would be talking about homophobia, and the next we would be planning an action." In a 1992 *Newsweek* article, Bratmobile drummer Molly Neuman echoed this: "We don't have a doctrine . . . there is no specific leader, no 10-point program." But within the constantly changing Riot Grrrl philosophy, some strong and specific solutions started to develop.

Girl Love

Riot grrrls advocated "girl love"—generating power through mutual support. A November 15, 1992, *New York Times* article reported, "The Riot Grrrl credo is that young women should take care of each other. 'This world doesn't teach us how to be truly cool to each other, and so we have to teach each other,' says a *Bikini Kill* manifesto . . . Riot Grrrl literature speaks out against the competition and jealousy that they feel society encourages among young women; the Riot Grrrls want to replace those attitudes with loyalty and support.' "

In the fanzine *GirlFrenzy*, riot grrrl Karen Ablaze relates the importance of this concept: "A bloke approached me . . . to ask me: 'What's this riot grrrl thing all about, then?' I replied: 'Girl Love.' 'But what's girl love?' he demanded. 'Well,' I began with a great deal of patience, 'part of girl love is self-love, because if you're a girl you have to love your own girlness before you can love anyone else's girlness. So, it's about loving yourself and then about loving other girls, and maybe even boys, too. It's about having a cool time, living out your dreams, doing those things you always wanted to do and finding other people who are into it too . . .' "

The Riot Grrrl–friendly band Team Dresch sums up the importance of the concept of mutual reliance in their song "She's Amazing." "She's amazing/her words save me . . . they say she's outspoken/many people will try to destroy her/but if she were to stop/I stop/we all stop." The idea is clear: The only way girls can be heard is if they speak out together.

Smashing Conventional Ideals of Beauty

Another feeling riot grrrls shared was a rebellion against beauty standards. Riot Grrrl encouraged women to take on whatever form of beauty was most comfortable for them. And unlike earlier feminists, they were not opposed to makeup and girly clothes—but only if this was a girl's choice, not something she felt she needed in order to be considered attractive. Kathleen Hanna explains in a *Punk Planet* interview, "A friend said to me, 'Why is it so subversive [revolutionary] to be beautiful in the traditional sense? I think it's much more subversive to create your own form of beauty and to set your own standards.' She's right." Again, the idea of doing it yourself—in this case, creating your own style of beauty as opposed to having it dictated to you by fashion magazines—is expressed.

Stardom and Fame

We are a culture in love with celebrities. Yet it only stands to reason that a philosophy that embraces the DIY credo would be against celebrity-worship. If you are doing it yourself, you are not worshipping other people. In an interview with *Princess* magazine, Hanna states, "I think part of the idea of being a star involves how it separates people: stars are superhuman, or 'real' people, and everyone else is supposed to be obsessed with their lives. Everyone else is supposed to be following what the 'real' people do, which means that everyone else is less than

One of Riot Grrrls' aims is to change the traditional standards of beauty espoused by popular culture.

real." Riot Grrrl valued all people—everyone's creations and all participation.

United Action!

Riot Grrrl is about action, DIY, revolution, and creating a new system. Action combined with the mutual support system of girl love did indeed make a lot happen. Girls started 'zines, bands, and comic books. They took action against sexual assault and abuse to create a world where they could be empowered on their own terms. By 1994, there were Riot Grrrl chapters all over the world, including the United States, England, and Canada.

The story of Karen Ablaze is just one example of how the spirit of Riot Grrrl traveled far beyond the Olympia and Washington, DC, scenes where it started. Ablaze started a Riot Grrrl chapter in the United Kingdom. While she had been creating her magazine, *Ablaze!*, for about five years, she still felt that, surrounded by men in her workplace, she was not free to express her feminist views. She heard about "something called Riot Grrrl, a girl punk rock movement in America." She got in touch with a chapter in London and was encouraged to start a chapter in her hometown of Leeds. So she did.

The girls who joined Ablaze's chapter started a fanzine. They put on shows, formed bands, and created more 'zines. "This is how I felt girl love turn into girl action," Ablaze says. One such action was the creation of a music and activism event. "The idea was to get a load of musical equipment in one place and give girls the chance to try stuff out, to get comfortable with the idea of playing guitar or whatever without criticism or expectations," Ablaze says. "[We] had workshops for various instruments and voice and songmaking, too. On another floor there was a fanzine workshop, as well as a putting-on-gigs workshop, an extensive girlzine stall and a rape crisis information point. It's like we've grown so much together and spread the fever to our friends as well as kept it moving, despite the tide of opinion that says we should not dare to be Riot Grrrls."

Ablaze, reflecting on her experiences as a riot grrrl, continues, "It looks as if the girls now involved are those who would have been active anyway, but that's not really true. Riot Grrrl has changed both those of us who were really active but wanted more . . . and those of us who hadn't really started doing this, but wanted to, and this provided the spark, the encouragement, the energy, the information, the networks."

Chapter Three

Women Who Rocked Before

There were women who represented what Riot Grrrl came to be long before the movement existed. Not surprisingly, many of them came out of the punk rock movement of the late 1970s, a time when women were allowed to freely participate. And these women were not forgotten by riot grrrls. "Although original female punks had mostly fallen from mainstream rock's collective memory, their records had continued to circulate underground, secretly inciting a new generation of young women," notes *Trouble Girls* editor, Barbara O'Dair. "There are now an astounding number of women playing in bands and having more success than ever. But it was that first wave of girl punks, with their angst-venting screams and gouged-out guitars, who provided today's female performers with something men take for granted: a legacy."

Exene (Christine) Cervenka fronted legendary punk group X.

Though many riot grrrl–like women from these early days do not, and never have, identified with the Riot Grrrl movement (or thought of them as feminists), they helped set the stage for grrrls. The following are just a few standout examples.

Exene Cervenka

The lead singer, songwriter, and namesake of the legendary Los Angeles punk band X, Exene (Christine) Cervenka is a prolific artist who always seems to float just below the surface of stardom. A poet from her early days in the West Coast punk scene, Cervenka became the lead singer of X after meeting future

Joan Jett influenced a generation of punk girls through both her music and her unique personal style.

bandmate John Doe at a poetry workshop. He encouraged her to make her poem "I'm Coming Over" into a song. She agreed, under the condition that she could sing it. Cervenka then became and remained the lead singer of the band. (The song "I'm Coming Over" appears on the album *Wild Gift*.)

Cervenka's personal style was also influential. With her tousled, long black locks streaked with blonde, and her trashy dressiness, she set a disheveled feminine standard that many a punk girl happily followed. She further perpetuated her unique fashion and sense of décor by opening, with John Rocker, the Los Angeles retail store "You've Got Bad Taste" (which closed after four years in business).

Seemingly less interested in the bright lights of fame than being true to her creative nature, Cervenka, after the breakup of X, has worked nonstop, creating spoken word recordings, books, and solo musical ventures and even forming another band with former X drummer DJ Bonebreak.

Joan Jett

An early fan of punk rock, Joan Jett had always wanted to play guitar. After a short stint with a guitar teacher who was not interested in teaching her the rock 'n' roll songs she wanted to play, Jett taught herself. Then, at the young age of sixteen, she became a member of the all-girl band the Runaways. Though they did gain some fame and are now seen as an important footnote in women's rock history, the Runaways were not treated very well nor were they understood. "I didn't understand people's reactions and why they thought it was so strange for women to play music," says Jett in *Angry Women in Rock*. "There were people who looked at us like we had seven heads . . . I wonder how many women actually looked at what we were doing in the Runaways and said, 'Hey, that's great.' Or, 'You make me feel stronger.' Because it seemed like the Runaways had a mostly male audience, waiting to see us take our clothes off or something—that's what they expected us to do."

After the Runaways broke up, Jett went on to front her own band, Joan Jett and the Blackhearts. After receiving twenty-three rejection letters from major and independent record labels, Jett decided to start her own label, Blackheart Records. Joan Jett and the Blackhearts went on to gain enormous popularity, recording several top ten hits, including "I Love Rock and Roll" and "Crimson and Clover."

Jett has gone on to work with Kathleen Hanna, producing some of Bikini Kill's recordings, writing music with Hanna, and playing guitar on the 1994 Bikini Kill release *Rebel Girl*. In *Angry Women in Rock*, Jett discusses her supportive relations with Hanna and other young female musicians, "It's a reciprocal sort of thing, which has led to us knowing each other and being able to work together." She also expresses her support for the

Riot Grrrl movement: "I think there have to be women out there who are willing to get in people's faces, just to let them know that women exist. If you read some of the 'zines that [riot grrrls] put out, you see that they're writing about incest and rape and all the other things that don't get talked about with women and teenage girls. These subjects get swept under the rug, and nobody wants to deal with them, because they're 'icky.' But something like rape or incest is a heavy subject for somebody that it happened to. So I think that's a really healthy outlet."

Poly Styrene

Vocalist and songwriter Poly Styrene (Marion Elliot) formed, fronted, and penned all songs for the late 1970s British band X-Ray Spex. Known for her trademark braced teeth and ear-piercing screech, Styrene's lyrics mocked conventional thinking. She brought into question a society of mindless consumerism. *Trouble Girls* editor O'Dair notes that Styrene "railed against the way capitalism made us all commodities."

Unfortunately, after some notable success, the band itself was on its way to becoming the very thing that Styrene wailed against. "[Styrene] had become part of the mass marketing of punk rebellion, and she knew it. After nearly suffering a breakdown, Poly broke up the band and went in search of a more spiritually connected way of life, eventually joining the Hare Krishnas," notes *Trouble Girls*.

Marion Elliot, aka Poly Styrene *(center)*, with late '70s punk band X-Ray Spex.

Indeed, without the inspiration of Styrene, who left X-Ray Spex in 1979, the band was clearly done. But Styrene continued to write lyrics and record solo material into the mid-1980s. Then, in a surprise move, Styrene got X-Ray Spex back together, and in 1995 they recorded *Conscious Consumer*.

The Slits

The Slits were it: They were the very first all-girl punk rock band. Formed in 1976 in London, they set a standard, especially for women, for just getting out there and making noise. As original drummer Palmolive (Paloma) states about the early intent of the Slits,

"Anything we could do to shock people, we were into. We couldn't play, we didn't pretend that we played." In true grrrl style, she goes on to say, "We just basically wanted to be whatever we wanted to be, do the things we wanted to do when we wanted to."

Well known for a unique and distinctly "unfeminine" style, the band was led by fourteen-year-old Ari Up (Arianna Forster), who had "wild, matted hair and sometimes liked to wear her underwear over her pants," according to *Trouble Girls*. The band's chaotic, reggae-influenced rhythms and uncompromising attitude have influenced many young women. As Jill Cunniff of the band Luscious Jackson recalls in *Trouble Girls*, "There was a time in my life when the Slits were the epitome, the ultimate, the coolest of the cool. They were everything I wanted from life."

The Riot Grrrl movement lives on today through bands like Sleater-Kinney.

Chapter Four

Where Are They Today?

Riot Grrrl flourished in the early 1990s. But what has come of the movement since then? Some say it has died. But what does that mean? And is it true that Riot Grrrl is dead?

If "dead" means that the spirit of Riot Grrrl is no longer a motivating force for women and girls, this is not true. If dead means that there is no more activity in the name of Riot Grrrl, this, too, is untrue. If dead means that the original creators of the movement are no longer involved in Riot Grrrl—that the movement has splintered and changed shape—this is true. True, too, is the fact that the original wave of enthusiasm that caught the attention of the media and general public has passed. As stated in *Trouble Girls*: "Many Riot Grrrl founders have moved on to other things, although chapters still meet in the United States and

Britain. The Riot Grrrl spirit of insurrection [rebellion] continues to inspire women to band together and make music." In fact, Riot Grrrl lives on in many ways.

In the Name of Riot Grrrl in the New Millennium

Today, numerous Riot Grrrl chapters remain active in the United States, a few are sprinkled throughout Canada, and some continue to meet in the United Kingdom. The Washington, DC, Riot Grrrl Web page guest book—the only currently active part of the Web site—posted this on February 19, 2000: "The European grrrls are just starting the riot and the Austrian grrrls have recently formed a chapter." Based on these accounts, the riot is alive and well.

In the true spirit of the movement, the New Jersey Web site says, "We are about teaching the world, old and young, male and female, about girl issues: equality, individuality, safety from victimization . . . We're about respecting ourselves." And the Cincinnati site posts a strong mission statement: "We are tired of waiting for someone else to start a revolution. We are going to do it ourselves. We want to listen, learn, talk, and help each other."

There is still a place for girls who want to call themselves riot grrrls. Girls continue to create this movement, banding together to keep the aggressive,

DIY spirit alive. For many girls, Riot Grrrl continues to be a source of strength from which they feed. And as long as any girl wishes to call herself a riot grrrl, the movement continues. Any girl can start a chapter. Any girl can start a 'zine. Any girl can get her friends together and start a band and say anything she wants to say.

Riot Grrrl today is not the same Riot Grrrl that Kathleen Hanna and the other Olympia and Washington, DC, feminists created. But isn't that what was supposed to happen? From the very beginning, Riot Grrrl was something that every girl could define for herself and the other girls with whom she united. The fact that this aggressive form of feminism continues to speak to and empower teenage girls proves that the Riot Grrrl movement is anything but dead.

The Legacy

What cannot be ignored is that the influence of Riot Grrrl has spread well beyond the movement. The Riot Grrrl movement inspired a lot of cultural and political action. The ideals central to Riot Grrrl have had a distinct influence on numerous women and on feminism in the new millennium.

This spirit can be felt in the music of new bands, one of the standouts being Sleater-Kinney. In the June 18, 2000, *New York Times* article about the band, vocalist and guitarist Corin Tucker reflects on the impact Riot Grrrl had on her. She comments on seeing the band Bikini Kill: "It was the first time I had seen feminism translated into an emotional language . . . For young women to be doing that, basically teenagers on stage, to be taking that kind of stance, that kind of power, was blowing people's minds. And it totally blew my mind. I was like, 'OK, that's it, that's it for me.'" And Sleater-Kinney have carried the Riot Grrrl torch well. The *Times* article goes on to say, "Their music is almost never played on commercial radio, and for good reason—like the Sex Pistols' music, it is so strong, so quick, so far-reaching, it makes nearly everything that today might surround it on the radio feel cowardly."

Riot Grrrl has also distinctly influenced the printed word. Many of those involved in creating their own 'zines, and others who have been inspired by the idea of self-publishing, have gone on to make it their profession. As a result, there are now a growing number of self-published feminist magazines such as *Bust*, *Moxie*, *Bitch*, and *Fabula*. All of these magazines pay homage to the Riot Grrrl movement. They continue to create female-defined worlds—the original goal of Riot Grrrl. This is reflected in *Bitch*'s mission statement: "Feminism is routinely ridiculed in the news and entertainment media, its tenets distorted by the willful ignorance of writers and commentators who insist that feminists have gotten everything we ever wanted and we should stop whining already . . . *Bitch* was founded on the impulse to give a voice to the vast numbers of us who know in our heart that these images are false, and want something to replace them."

Riot Grrrl also bolstered the popularity of another print medium, comic books. In *From Girls to Grrrlz*, author Trina Robbins observes, "By the 1990s, women . . . empowered by Riot Grrrlz, adopted the 'zine as a perfect medium in which to share their personal stories, rants . . . and comics." From Sarah Dyer's *Action Girl* to Jessica Abel's *Art Babe*, Diane DiMassi's *Hothead Paisan* to Ariel Schrag's *Potential*, the number of comics created by women and featuring primarily women characters is growing. Sarah Dyer's introduction to *Action Girl* states: "Remember, action is everything . . . Be an action girl (or boy) . . . go out and do something with all that positive energy!"

And then there is the Internet, an arena widely used to share and express ideas, and meet up with like-minded individuals. Riot Grrrl–like sites are all over the Web and serve as a forum for posting band information, essays, journals, guest books, poetry, and art. Sites such as generationgrrl.com, chickclick.com, coolgrrrls.com, and riotgrrl.com all perpetuate the DIY feminist philosophy. For younger girls, there is gURL.com, through which many Riot Grrrl–like Web sites have been launched. Many of these sites offer riot grrrls e-mail accounts of their own.

The Riot Grrrl concept of unity, or girl love, among women and girls continues in these new entities as well. Sarah Dyer promotes other women comic artists

Riot Grrrl inspired young women to start their own comics, like Sarah Dyer's *Action Girl*.

in *Action Girl* and a recent issue of *Bitch* featured Dyer. The Spring 1999 issue of *Bust* featured Kathleen Hanna. Ads for *Fabula* can be found in *Bitch*. And almost every Web site has links to other like-minded sites. *Bust*'s Web site alone posts over 200 links to female-oriented sites. The creation of a supportive women-defined community continues.

Coming of Age

Riot Grrrl has taken on a variety of forms, but there is a common thread running through them all: the creation of a place for women, defined by women, that allows women to unite and support each other. There are teenagers who carry on in the name of Riot Grrrl, influenced by the movement to be themselves, take action, unite with other girls, and have confidence in their abilities. They continue to challenge social constructs that are destructive and limiting, and instead make choices that are liberating.

Then there are the founders—most of whom do not participate in Riot Grrrl any longer—and those influenced by the movement's early years. They have entered adulthood and continue the revolution, integrating the DIY philosophy into their lifestyle. Many continue to take action, be creative, and live a life in which their earlier ideals remain uncompromised. They continue to voice their "moanings" and define their revolution. By setting an example, they continue to give young women inspiration. They respond to the challenge posed by *Newsweek*: What happens "when [Riot Grrrl] hits the adult real world?" Riot Grrrl continues to grow, become more pervasive, and develop into a respected and well-recognized women's movement. Riot Grrrl is not just a fashion trend, but a lasting expression of powerful femininity.

Even the media finally seem to be "getting it." The June 18, 2000, *New York Times* article, paraphrasing Sleater-Kinney's Corin Tucker, states, "You too can stand up and speak in a town square, even if you have to create the town square yourself."

Riot Grrrl has had a tremendous influence all over the world. It has given girls and women who wish to live outside of the system—a system that they did not create and that does not allow them to fully express themselves—a place to exist. And there are no signs that Riot Grrrl is near the end. In fact, it may not be too far-fetched to believe that Riot Grrrl will reach its "ultimate goal." As Kathleen Hanna states in *Punk Planet*, "We change the entire system."

Glossary

capitalism An economic system in which private individuals or corporations own businesses and in which prices are dependent on market competition.

confrontational Able or willing to address difficult or controversial issues.

feminism Activity on behalf of women's rights and interests.

feminists People whose belief system supports the actions and interests of women.

first wave feminism The suffragist or voting rights movement during the late nineteenth and early twentieth centuries.

marginalization The act of excluding a group or a school of thought from mainstream society.

misrepresent To give misleading or false information about someone or something.

patriarchy   A society based on the father or male as leader or supreme force.

philosophy   The beliefs and attitudes of a group or an individual.

punk rock   A social movement that began in the late 1970s.

revolution   The overthrowing of a current system. Or, a fundamental change in the way something is thought about.

riot   Public disorder.

second wave feminism   The movement for women's rights during the 1960s and 1970s that called for an end to discrimination based on sex.

separatist   One who supports the separation of one group from another.

subculture   A group that identifies itself as being outside the norm.

victimization   The act of making someone a victim.

'zine (or fanzine)   Hand-made, self-published magazine with a relatively small distribution.

For More Information

Bitch Magazine
2765 16th Street
San Francisco, CA 94103
(415) 864-6671
Web site: http://www.bitchmagazine.com

BUST Magazine
P. O. Box 1016
Cooper Station
New York, NY 10276
Web site: http://www.bust.com

Fabula Magazine
5337 College Avenue, #301
Oakland, CA 94618
Web site: http://www.fabulamag.com

Feminist Majority
8105 West Third Street
Los Angeles, CA 90048
(323) 651-0495
Web site: http://www.feminist.org

Moxie Magazine
1230 Glen Avenue
Berkeley, CA 94708
(510) 540-5510
Web site: http://www.moxiemag.com

National Organization for Women
733 15th Street NW, 2nd Floor
Washington, DC 20005
(202) 628-8NOW [8669]
Web site: http://www.now.org

Web Sites

Action Girl
http://www.houseoffun.com/action

Chick Click
http://www.chickclick.com

Cool Grrrls
http: //www.coolgrrrls.com

Generation Grrl
http://www.generationgrrl.com

gURL
http://www.gURL.com

Riot Grrl Online
http://www.riotgrrl.com

Rockin' Rina's Women of 1970's Punk
http://www.comnet.ca/~rina

For Further Reading

Archer, Jules. *Breaking Barriers: The Feminist Revolution from Susan B. Anthony to Margaret Sanger to Betty Friedan.* New York: Viking, 1991.

Friedan, Betty. *The Feminine Mystique.* 3rd ed. New York: W. W. Norton, 1997.

Green, Karen, and Tristan Taormino, eds. *A Girl's Guide to Taking Over the World: Writings from the Girl Zine Revolution.* New York: St. Martin's Griffen, 1997.

Hooks, Bell. *Feminist Theory: From Margin to Center.* 2nd ed. Cambridge, MA: South End Press, 2000.

Juno, Andrea. *Angry Women in Rock.* New York: Juno Books, 1996.

Leblanc, Lauraine. *Pretty in Punk: Girls' Gender Resistance in a Boys' Subculture.* New Brunswick, NJ: Rutgers University Press, 1999.

O'Dair, Barbara, ed. *Trouble Girls: The Rolling Stone Book of Women in Rock.* New York: Random House, 1997.

Robbins, Trina. *Girls to Grrrlz: A History of Women's Comics from Teens to Zines.* San Francisco: Chronicle Books, 1999.

Index

Index

Acknowledgments

My thanks go out to Amy Vreeland, Katie Stence, Kerry Callahan, and riot grrrls Amber Gynarchy and Melanie for keepin' it real.

About the Author

Chérie Turner is a writer and editor who lives in San Francisco.

Photo Credits

Cover © Stephen Simpson/FPG International. P. 2 © Andrew Lichtenstein/The Image Works; p. 6 © Corbis; p. 9 © The Image Bank; p. 11 © Corbis; p. 13 © Ebet Roberts; p. 17 © Pat Graham; pp. 21, 44 © The Everett Collection; p. 22 © AP/Worldwide; p. 27 © Tammy Rae Carland; p. 35 © Robert Bertoia/The Everett Collection; p. 36 © Thomas Forget; p. 39 © Ken Marcus; p. 40 © Kraig Geiger/The Everett Collection; p. 46 © Peter DaSilva; p. 52–53 © Sarah Dyer.

Layout

Geri Giordano